The World of Composers

Bach

Greta Cencetti

PETER BEDRICK BOOKS

McGraw-Hill
Children's Publishing
A Division of The McGraw·Hill Companies

This edition published in the United States in 2002 by
Peter Bedrick Books, an imprint of
McGraw-Hill Children's Publishing,
A Division of The McGraw-Hill Companies
8787 Orion Place
Columbus, Ohio 43240

www.MHkids.com

ISBN 1-58845-467-3

Library of Congress Cataloging-in-Publication Data

Cencetti, Greta.
Bach / Greta Cencetti.
p. cm. -- (The world of composers)
Summary: Describes the life and career of the early eighteenth-century
German composer and organist Johann Sebastian Bach.
ISBN 1-58845-467-3
1. Bach, Johann Sebastian, 1685-1750--Juvenile literature. 2. Composers—
Germany—Biography—Juvenile literature. [1. Bach, Johann Sebastian,
1685-1750. 2. Composers.] I. Title. II. Series.

ML3930.B2 C46 2002
780'.92--dc21
[B]
2001052423

10 9 8 7 6 5 4 3 2 1 CHRT 06 05 04 03 02 01

Printed in China.

The World of Composers

Bach

Greta Cencetti

PETER BEDRICK BOOKS

Contents

Eisenach

Chapter 1
Bach's Early Childhood

Johann Sebastian Bach (pronounced bahk) was born on March 21, 1685, in Eisenach, a small village in northern Germany.

Bach was the son of Johann Ambrosius Bach and Maria Elisabeth Lämmerhirt. Young Johann had three brothers and a sister who survived infancy.

The Bach family came from a long line of musicians. Bach's father served as church organist in Eisenach.

Bach's father usually played the organ with his twin brother. When the brothers gathered in the church with all their children and musical instruments, they looked like an entire orchestra.

1650

1700

Chapter 2
The Choir Boy and Violinist

Bach had a happy early childhood, filled with love and music. When he was only nine years old, though, Bach's parents died and his life changed. Young Bach and his brother, Johann Jacob, went to live with their older brother, Johann Christoph, and his wife in a nearby village, called Ohrdruf. Like Bach, Johann Christoph was an organist. Young Bach learned about music and repairing pipe organs from his brother. He would often sit in the moonlight writing musical scores. At that time, organists did not earn much money, so the Bach family had to watch what they spent.

When Bach was 15, he left his brother's household and set off with his friend, Georg Erdmann, who also loved music. They moved to a nearby town called Lüneberg. There, the two friends earned a living as members of an all-boys' choir.

As he and Georg grew older, though, their voices grew too deep for singing in the choir.

Young Bach learned to play a variety of musical instruments. He especially enjoyed playing the violin. The choir director noticed his abilities and introduced Bach to the violinist of St. Michael's Church. At St. Michael's, Bach mastered the organ and soon became the church organist.

Chapter 3
Organist and Choir Director

Bach traveled throughout Germany. In 1702, he helped to inspect a new organ at the "Neue-Kirche" (New Church) in Arnstadt. This led to a job as the pipe organist and choir director. Bach accepted the job because he enjoyed hearing the wide range of sounds that the new pipe organ could make.

Unfortunately, when Bach accepted the job, it meant that Andreas Börner, the current organist at the New Church, would have to be fired. An agreement was eventually reached that Börner would be given other employment at the church.

Chapter 4
The Traveling Composer

While Bach was at the New Church, he allowed his cousin Maria and another woman to join the choir. During Bach's time, it was not the custom for women to be in the church choir. The people in the congregation became angry with him.

Bach did not wish to stay in Arnstadt, so he married Maria, and they moved to a town called Mühlhausen. Though Bach was well-liked in Mühlhausen, the couple left shortly afterwards for the town of Weimar. There, Bach displayed his ability to play the organ for Duke Wilhelm Ernst. He hoped that he would become the choir director at Duke Wilhelm Ernst's chapel.

Unfortunately, Bach found out that the Duke had already hired a choir director. Bach packed his things, with plans to move his family to yet another city. This made the Duke very angry. He had Bach arrested and put in prison for nearly a month.

After his release from prison, Bach and his family moved to the town of Köthen. There, he met the young Prince Leopold, who hired Bach as his choir director in 1717.

Chapter 5
A Love of Religious Music

*T*hree years later, Bach's wife, Maria, died from an unknown illness, leaving behind four children. The other three Bach children had died in infancy. Maria died while Bach was away for two months with Prince Leopold. He returned to find her dead and recently buried.

It is thought that he composed the great d-minor *Chaconne* in her memory. He also wrote other inspirational religious music during this time. He remained as choir director in Köthen.

Within a year, Bach met a young woman named Anna. They were soon married. He and Anna had 13 children. Now there were 17 children in the Bach family!

In the evenings, the family gathered in the music room in their home to sing and play music together. Anna was also a talented musician. She was especially skilled at playing a keyboard instrument called the clavichord.

The clavichord was an early keyboard instrument in which the keys were simple levers, like a seesaw. When the player pressed the key down, the other end went up. This struck the string with a small metal blade, called a *tangent*. The clavichord had a soft, melodic sound so it was usually used as a personal instrument, not as a concert instrument.

Chapter 6
The Music Director of Leipzig

In 1729, Bach was invited to become the music director of Leipzig. This was an important job in a large German city, and with it came more responsibilities.

As the music director of Leipzig, Bach wrote songs for religious ceremonies, led the church choir, and played the organ for important events. He also had to make sure that the pipe organ was in good working order.

Bach came to know other musicians in Leipzig. He stayed there for the rest of his life.

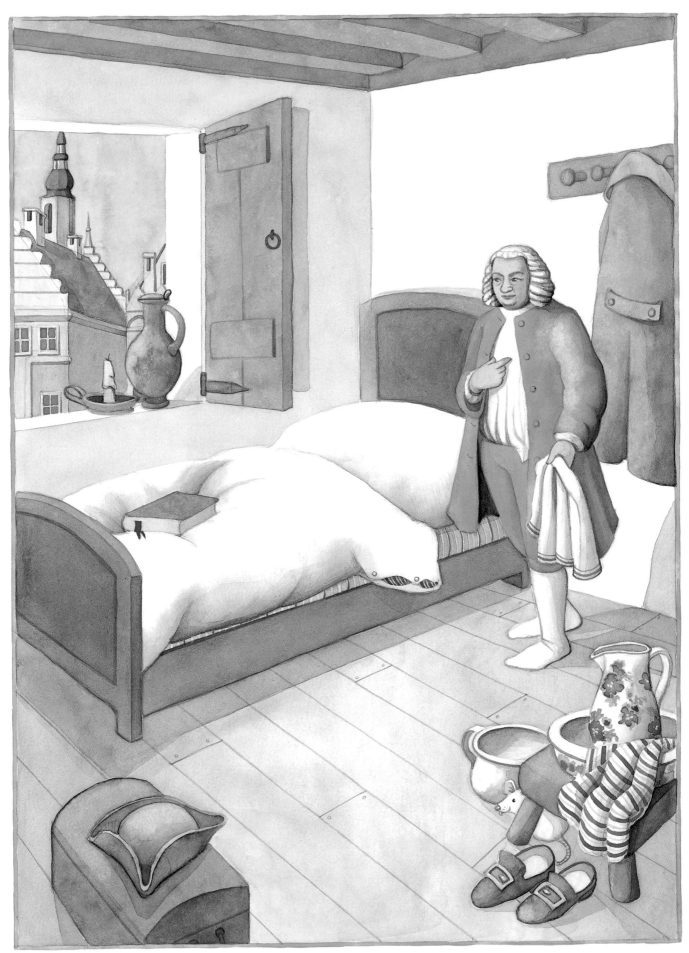

Chapter 7

An Important Invitation

In 1747, Bach was asked to travel to Potsdam to play for Frederick the Great. Frederick was one of the most powerful men in the world at that time. He loved music, played the flute, and composed. Bach's son, Carl Phillip Emannuel, already worked for Frederick the Great. Bach stayed at an inn in Potsdam, awaiting his invitation to the palace. When Frederick found out that Bach had arrived, he sent for him immediately. Frederick the Great showed Bach several keyboard instruments, including a very early type of piano, which had just been invented.

After Bach played for him, Frederick the Great was deeply moved. He, in turn, played one of his own themes on the harpsichord for Bach. Frederick asked Bach to write a fugue on it, a musical composition in which one or two themes have voices entering at different times.

Bach wrote a three-voice fugue. Frederick thought it was so good that he asked Bach to compose a very difficult, six-voice fugue. Bach told Frederick that he could, but that a composition written for a king deserved more thought. He knew he would do a better job if he could work on it at home and write it out on paper.

Bach promised to set the theme in many different ways and to present them in a printed book to Frederick. After Bach returned to Leipzig he did just that, and called the work *The Musical Offering*.

Chapter 8
Bach's Last Days

Later in his life, Bach wrote a variety of musical pieces for many different instruments. Still completely devoted to music, he continued to compose inspired religious pieces.

Toward the end of his life, Bach wrote a composition called *Goldberg Variations*, about a man he knew who had difficulty sleeping. The song was so calm and soothing that the man listened to it at night to help him go to sleep. It is said that the man was so grateful, he gave Bach a full cup of gold coins to thank him.

Johann Sebastian Bach died from a stroke in the summer of 1750. He left behind a great gift of original and powerful musical creations.

Introduction to the Organ

Johann Sebastian Bach was a master of the pipe organ. The development of the pipe organ, sometimes called the "king of instruments," can be traced back to the 3rd century B.C. Large pipe organs can have thousands of pipes, and can make many different types of sound, often sounding like flutes, oboes, and ancient instruments not in use today. In a way, the organ is an early synthesizer, an electronic device that makes and controls sound.

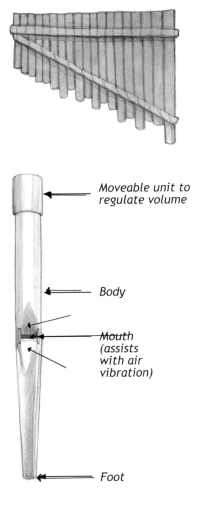

Moveable unit to regulate volume

Body

Mouth (assists with air vibration)

Foot

The kind of organ pipe shown here operates on the same principle as the flute: to get enough air into the pipes, a foot-operated pump (like a fireplace bellows) was used. One of Bach's duties in the morning before church was to go to the jail and get someone to pump the organ. Today, no one has to pump the organ: air is supplied by an electric fan. In some cases, the organ pipes themselves have been replaced by a computer that synthesizes their sound, which is played back through loudspeakers.

Like a piano, organs have keyboards—sometimes three, four, or five of them—allowing the player to put different sounds on each keyboard and quickly going from one sound to the other. The organ also has a keyboard, called a *pedal clavier,* which is played with the feet. In addition, the organ also has a large number of buttons and switches that allow the player to "program" different combinations of sounds. Playing the organ takes a good deal of coordination.